Weather Wise

Sunshine

Helen Cox Cannons

Heinemann
LIBRARY
Chicago, Illinois

Edited by Siân Smith and John-Paul Wilkins
Designed by Philippa Jenkins and Peggie Carley
Picture research by Ruth Blair
Production by Victoria Fitzgerald
Originated by Capstone Global Library Ltd
Printed in the United States of America in
North Mankato, MN. 102014 008556RP

Library of Congress Cataloging in Publication Data
Cataloging-in-publication information is on file with the Library
of Congress.
ISBN 978-1-4846-0547-9 (hardcover)
ISBN 978-1-4846-0557-8 (paperback)
ISBN 978-1-4846-0572-1 (eBook PDF)

Photo Credits
Dreamstime: Gpointstudio, 19, Logoboom, 16; Getty Images:
Maria Pavlova/E+, cover; iStockphoto: Alexander Chernyakov,
9, 23 (bottom), Kali Nine LLC, 14, konradlew, 10, skynesher, 21,
Squaredpixels, 5, zeljkosantrac, 18; NASA: 12; Shutterstock:
Africa Studio, 22 (sunscreen), bddigitalimages, 8, 23 (middle),
hddigital, 6, 23 (top), Ivonne Wierink, 22 (hat), koosen, 22 (ball),
Ljupco Smokovski, 22 (chair), Marques, 22 (duck), oneo, 4,
Patrizia Tilly, 15, Stephen Lew, 17, Sunny Forest, 11, Tom Wang, 20,
Vibrant Image Studio, 7

We would like to thank John Horel for his invaluable help in the
preparation of this book.

Every effort has been made to contact copyright holders of
material reproduced in this book. Any omissions will be rectified
in subsequent printings if notice is given to the publisher.

Contents

What Is Sunshine? 4

The Sun 12

Sunshine and the Seasons 14

Sunshine Around the World 16

Staying Safe in the Sun 18

How Does Sunshine Help Us? 20

Sunshine Quiz 22

Picture Glossary 23

Index 24

Notes for Parents and Teachers 24

What Is Sunshine?

Sunshine is light from the Sun.

Sunshine is very bright. Sunshine feels warm on your skin.

The Sun **rises** in the morning.
Then it becomes light outside.

During the day, the Sun moves across the sky.

The Sun **sets** in the evening.
Then it becomes dark outside.

You cannot see the Sun at night.
The Sun moves below the **skyline**.

The Sun heats the ocean.

The Sun heats the land.

The Sun

The Sun is a burning ball of gas.

Sunshine feels warm because it comes from the Sun.

Sunshine and the Seasons

Earth is closer to the Sun in summer.
Summer days can be hot.

Earth is farther away from the Sun
in winter. Winter days can be cold.

Sunshine Around the World

equator

Countries near the **equator** have very strong sunshine. These countries are often warm all year round.

Countries far from the equator have very weak sunshine. These countries are cold all year round.

Staying Safe in the Sun

Sunshine can burn your skin. Wear sunscreen to stay safe in the Sun.

Never look at the Sun. It can damage your eyes.

How Does Sunshine Help Us?

Sunshine helps plants grow.

Sunshine makes people feel happy!

Sunshine Quiz

Which of these things will keep you safe in the Sun?

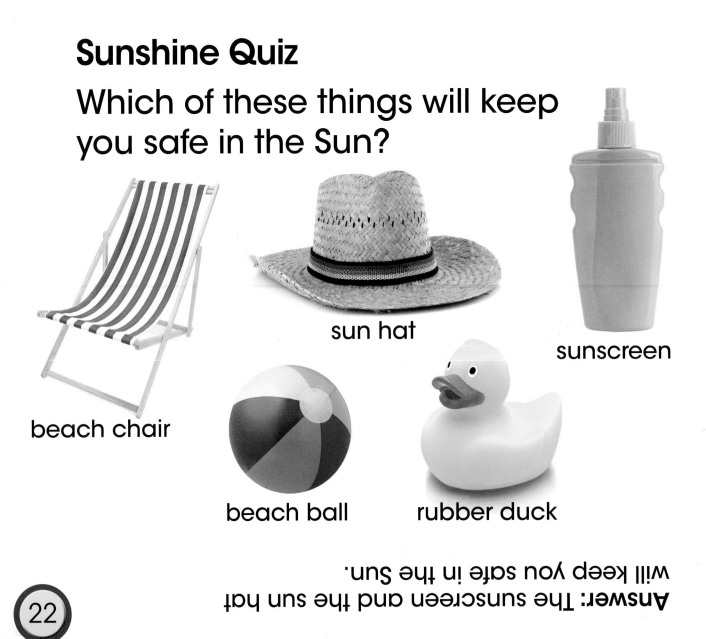

sun hat

sunscreen

beach chair

beach ball

rubber duck

Answer: The sunscreen and the sun hat will keep you safe in the Sun.

Picture Glossary

 **equator** imaginary circle around the middle of Earth

 **rise** to come up

 **set** to go down

 **skyline** the place where land and sky meet

Index

equator 16, 17, 23

skyline 9, 23

summer 14

winter 15

Notes for Parents and Teachers

Before Reading
Assess background knowledge. Ask: What is sunshine? Where does sunshine come from? How does sunshine help us?

After Reading
Recall and reflection: Ask children if their ideas about sunshine at the beginning were correct. What else do they wonder about?

Sentence knowledge: Ask children to look at page 16. How many sentences are on this page? How can they tell?

Word recognition: Have children point at the word *warm* on page 5. Can they also find it on page 13?